Make Money by Decluttering Your Home

How Supplement the Income from Your Job or Social Security without Spending a Fortune

Richard G Lowe, Jr

Make Money by Decluttering Your Home

How Supplement the Income from Your Job or Social Security without Spending a Fortune

Earn Money from Home Series #2

Published by The Writing King
www.thewritingking.com

Make Money by Decluttering Your Home

Cover Artist: theamateurzone

ASIN: B01HAK03UY
ISBN: 978-1-943517-81-7 (Hardcover)
ISBN: 978-1-943517-80-0 (Paperback)
ISBN: 978-1-943517-37-4 (eBook)

Table of Contents

Table of Contents

Introduction

Life can be very hard sometimes, especially when it comes to money. There never seems to be enough to go around, and this is even more apparent when you are trying to support a family, send your kids to school, pay off the bills, get a house, and build up savings for those rainy days.

If only there were a way to make some extra income, something that wasn't a scam or required a significant investment. If only you could find something, somewhere to make a few extra thousand dollars. Wouldn't that be helpful? Could you use a thousand, two thousand or even three thousand dollars? Wouldn't it be great to get the kind of income every single month?

There are so many "programs" which promise instant money with little effort if only you pay an initial sum of $997 plus $50 per month. None of them ever seem to pay off, even with all of the testimonials on their website from people claiming they've made hundreds of thousands or millions of dollars in little or no time. Does any of them really work?

And the training — much of this training is so expensive as to put it out of reach. Most of us don't have the luxury of having the money and time to take course after course, hoping for one of them to pay off.

Fortunately, there is a way that most people can make extra money from their home without a significant investment. It requires little to no training, and the equipment and supplies needed are inexpensive and easily obtainable.

Introduction

Many of us have accumulated large amounts of things over the years. We may have had hobbies and collections, but our interest faded as we grew older. For example, I collected stamps for many years, and eventually owned over one hundred thousand of them, carefully sorted in binders filling a bookshelf. Unfortunately, I lost interest decades ago, and the stamps no longer serve any purpose for me. They just take up space and need to be occasionally cleaned.

Quite a few of us have had children and continue to store old toys, kids items, baby cribs, and numerous other things in a closet or even a storage unit. Sometimes there's an emotional attachment to these articles since they are associated with our children, so we keep them locked even though they no longer serve any purpose in our lives.

Perhaps a friend or relative has passed on, and you've had to store their belongings in your home or storage. You don't want to throw out their stuff, but it costs money, space and time to keep it safe and secure.

Virtually everyone has stories such as this that they could tell.

All of this stuff is clutter, which are things that we own that we no longer need, never required in the first place, don't want, or don't know what to do with. Clutter takes up valuable space, and sometimes money to store, and serves no purpose at all. This junk seems so precious, so important that we don't want to throw it out.

There is an answer to clutter. It's an answer that works to help you make some extra money, and as you gain experience in doing so, you can leverage what you've learned into a second income that you can earn from home.

I'm talking about EBay, which is the largest online market in the world. Millions of people use EBay every day to buy and sell products of all kinds.

You can rummage through the clutter that you have already purchased, stuff you have stored in your closets, stacked on your bookcases, stuffed in your drawers, and jammed into rented storage units and turn it all into cash.

You just need to take the time and have the willpower to go through the junk, separate what you're going to keep and what you are going to sell, and then list them on EBay in such a way to attract buyers.

Sometimes the hardest part is parting with your stuff. After all, I'm sure you've hung too much of it for years or even decades. But really, is it doing you any good? Is that storage unit jammed with things that you haven't even looked at in two years and have moved with you all over the country for the last two decades actually helping you survive?

Just think of how much money you're spending storing items that you never use and no longer need. Consider how much time you spent packing, unpacking and moving clutter that serves no useful purpose in your life and the life of your family.

Wouldn't it be better to convert all of that stuff into cold hard cash?

Introduction

Could you use some of that money that you have tied up in clutter? Would it be useful to help you pay off some debts, pay for your children's schooling, or even go on a vacation?

The purpose of this book is to assist you to make some extra income by selling some or all of your clutter. Not only will this make you some money, but it will also help you feel happier and lighter.

For many people, the weight of their belongings can become overwhelming. All that stuff has to be stored, cataloged, examined, moved, moved again, packed, unpacked, dusted, cleaned and protected.

This focus on belongings can make people feel depressed, introverted, and un-trusting of others.

I know from personal experience that the time that I've taken to declutter my life and get rid of things that I own and don't need has been a very fulfilling and useful exercise.

I was amazed at how much better I felt — a little bit each day — as I sold off my clutter. In the beginning, it was rough because all of that stuff seemed so valuable, so important. So many memories were tied up in my belongings, so much energy and so much apparent value.

As I went through it all, listed it on EBay item by item, then sold everything and packed them up and shipped them to someone else, I felt like a weight was lifted from my shoulders. Life began to feel more fulfilling, and my focus changed to the future rather than the past.

On top of that, I felt good because I was taking things that had been hidden in closets and boxes and on bookshelves for decades, and sold them to someone who had uses for them. I felt good about moving the stuff along to new owners so they could get value from things that I had enjoyed in my past.

This book is the second volume in a series about how to make money over the web from home. The first book, called *How to Sell on eBay*, describes how to set up and use EBay to create a second income. The third volume, called *Make Money Using the Internet to Build a Second Income and Create your Own Business*, goes into detail about other options available to make an income off the web.

If you have never used EBay, then you should start by reading the first volume of the series, *How to Sell on eBay*, to learn the fundamentals.

This book, the one you're reading now, makes the assumption that you've already set up your EBay account and know how to use it. The focus is on how to confront your clutter and use the things you already own to make yourself money and build up the experience to start an ongoing EBay business. By using belongings that you've already paid for, you can enter the world of EBay as a seller without having to learn how to stock your store from other sources.

Besides, I have found, like I said earlier, the very act of decluttering my life has vastly improved my emotional state by eliminating the attention I had on my belongings.

At this point, after selling off a significant amount of my junk, the things that I own are the things that I really want or need.

Introduction

These are things that I currently collect or use, or are uplifting to me in the present.

I began selling on both Amazon and EBay. Each site has their advantages and disadvantages. At first, I favored Amazon since it seemed to be easier to confront than EBay, but after a while, I moved over to EBay because I found it to be less expensive and my products sold much quicker.

About six months before writing this book, I dove into EBay completely. My mindset had changed, and material items had become much less important to me. Besides, as I looked around my place, I realized that I had a lot of money tied up in clutter, and I could put that to better use in other areas of my life.

I began with my movie collection, followed by my role-playing games, video games, art, stamps, and many other things. In the past, I had made a $100 here and a $100 there selling things, now I was making $3,000 or $4,000 extra per month.

That kind of money came in very handy in paying off some debt and getting a little bit ahead.

The only way to begin is to begin. You have to start, and you have to start somewhere. I hope you find the information here to be a valuable guide for your decluttering adventures.

HOARDERS

Hoarders are beyond the scope of this book. These people hold onto things out of a compulsion, merely for the sake of owning them. I have known a few hoarders in my life, and they have accumulated immense piles of useless junk with little to no value.

In a particularly horrifying example, I visited someone who had piles of newspapers and other garbage reaching from the floor to the ceiling throughout their four-bedroom home, with narrow pathways threading here and there. These homes stank of rotting paper and garbage attracted insects and rats and were fire traps.

Those people are beyond the scope of this book. If you've ever known anyone with this compulsion, then you know that it's not something that's easily solvable.

Decluttering your Life

No matter what you're doing in your life, beginnings can be difficult. Decluttering is no exception to the rule; in fact, getting rid of many of the things that you have accumulated over the years or even decades can be harder than just about anything else you've ever done.

Most people hold onto things because they perceive these objects have a value of some kind or another. Their belongings give them a sense of ownership and comfort, and may even bring back memories. They often believe there is some value in keeping items which may prove to be valuable in the future.

Whatever the reason, most of the clutter in your life is subtracting from the quality of your life.

Just think of all the money that you have tied up in all of your clutter, and what you could do with that income right now. I found that imagining what I could with that money is a very effective way to overcome my personal barriers about removing the clutter.

Keep in mind that when you're selling your junk, you're listing it on EBay or another site such as Craigslist, and this means that you're holding onto the clutter until sold.

Thus, in this case, decluttering means creating an inventory, photographing and listing each item on EBay.

Decluttering your Life

It's important to have a system in place to record the location of items that you sell. Otherwise, you might find yourself frantically searching through boxes for that silver spoon that you listed on EBay two months ago and forgot about.

After my first sales, I searched for hours to find a book or DVD so that I could ship it to the buyer. Because of this, I came up with a system. At the bottom of each listing, I include a short code to describe the location of each item. For example, [LR-C1] means "Living Room, Cabinet 1." Other people create spreadsheets listing each item and their location.

I BOUGHT THIS STUFF FOR A REASON

One reason it's so hard to get rid of things is you purchased then —books, paintings, games or whatever — for a reason. They seemed important at the time, had some value to you, even if it was only momentarily.

As I was growing up, I was a voracious reader. I read everything I could get my hands on, and soon found that the local library didn't carry what I wanted; in fact, a few books had been censored with blacked-out passages. Because of that, I began accumulating my own library of books, and by the time I moved out from my parent's house at nineteen I had over five thousand in my collection.

On top of that, I was very introverted, had few friends, and my home life was hostile. All of these things served to cause books to become my friends, and I built up a lot of positive emotion regarding my collection.

Because of my emotional attachment, even the simple task of contemplating getting rid of any of them was difficult. After all, they had been my friends for so long; at some points in my life, they were my only companions. How could I get rid of any of them?

It took a week, but I finally went through them all and found one book, just one, that I thought I could live without. I brought that to the used bookstore and sold it for a fraction of what I paid. But I noticed something; I felt good. Selling that one book made me feel better for just a few minutes. I started to wonder, what would happen if I sold some more?

A week later I brought a box of books to the bookstore. It seemed in the intervening time about a dozen of them had become unimportant. I made quite a bit of money off of that sale since they were textbooks. These particular volumes seemed safe to sell since I wasn't going back to college.

I noticed that the act of selling these books made me feel excellent. I'd made an extra hundred bucks — which I desperately needed at the time — but more importantly, I felt lighter somehow, as if a burden had been removed.

I SPENT GOOD MONEY ON THIS STUFF

Another reason getting rid of clutter can be difficult is good money was spent to purchase those things. Over the years, you've probably accumulated thousands or tens of thousands of dollars of stuff which are now stored in your home, storage unit, possibly in your car, backyard, and anywhere else you can find.

Decluttering your Life

It's important to understand and come to terms with the fact that the money is already gone. It doesn't matter whether the purchase was right or not, the money is gone. In fact, you're spending even more money — if only because the stuff is taking up space — storing it and keeping it safe.

Years after selling those books, and after moving for the third time, I realized that there were thousands of books my collection that I was never going to read, or was never even going to look at again. However, here I was, packing everything all up in heavy boxes, paying movers by the pound to cart them all over town, and then unpacking them and organizing the books on bookshelves. On top of that, I had to clean them constantly, dust them, make sure they were in order, protect them, and so forth.

I had a realization that owning a library which, by that time, had grown to almost 10,000 books, was ridiculous. But I had to overcome the thought that I spent tens of thousands of dollars on them over the course of two decades. I knew that I would be selling everything at a loss — books rarely gain in value over the years — and that just seemed wrong. It took me quite a while to overcome that barrier.

Within a period of about six months, I cut my book collection in half and wound up getting rid of six full bookshelves. Not just the books, but the shelves themselves. That was quite an accomplishment, and I felt splendid.

SOMEDAY IT MIGHT BE VALUABLE
Sometimes we keep things because they might have value someday. I used to hear from my parents that they grew up in

the Great Depression, and they didn't have much. They kept everything, never knowing what they might need to survive.

This is another barrier that I needed to overcome, and you might need to confront it as well. We've all heard the story of the mother who threw out her son's comic books, thinking them to be of no value. Years later, her son found out that he could've sold that Superman #1 for a thousand bucks and his Spiderman comic at auction for tens of thousands of dollars.

The problem is that most of the things that we buy in our daily lives are never going to accumulate much value. While there might be one comic book in that stack that is worth a few hundred dollars after forty years, the truth is that the rest of them are probably wastepaper.

I found this out the hard way when I tried to sell my comic book collection. I'd held onto them for almost 20 years, and I had the thought that they must be worth some money. After all, aren't comic books always worth lots of money? Especially ones that are over twenty years old. I filled the entire back seat of my car with boxes of them — there must've been a thousand comics — and drove to the comic book store.

The dealer thumbed through them, making little tsk tsk noises, pulled out about a dozen, and offered me a total of a hundred dollars for those. I asked about the rest, and he said he'd take them off my hands for another hundred bucks. That was $100 for all but a dozen of the one thousand or so in my collection.

I learned a critical lesson that day — the whole mindset of "it might be worth something someday" is hogwash.

Yes, it is true that some items do gain value over the years. I bought a Dungeons & Dragons first edition role-playing game for around $10 in 1978 and wound up on selling it on EBay years later for $500. So it does happen, but these exceptions don't excuse keeping everything that you've ever owned.

IT BRINGS BACK MEMORIES

Occasionally, I find that I keep stuff because "it brings back memories." Those memories are not always pleasurable, yet for some reason, I hold things to "remind me" for whatever reason.

I've known many people that hold onto pictures of old boyfriends or girlfriends, even when the breakups were rough. Some of us hold onto toys from childhood: a doll collection from when they were a young girl or the baseball cards they so diligently collected as a boy in the sixth grade.

Yet over the years, all of these things get packed away into boxes, stuffed inside drawers, or collect dust on bookshelves.

One day, I was digging through boxes of my stuff, and I realized these things made me feel depressed every time I looked at them. There were bad memories associated with these things. I'd been hanging on to belongings from my childhood, my marriage, and other points in my life because they "had memories"; yet those memories were not good, or at least the emotions they brought to mind were not helpful.

I asked myself the question, "why am I keeping things that make me feel bad?"

I couldn't come up with an answer to that, so I decided that everything that I owned that caused me to feel angry, depressed, sad, and so forth needed to go. This was before the days of the web, so I sold them to friends and local thrift stores.

Some of the objects made me feel so bad that I simply threw them in the trash can. One or two belongings triggered such amounts of anger that I took great joy in smashing them with a sledgehammer in the middle of the driveway.

I felt extraordinarily good when I finished getting rid of all of the objects in my life that brought forth unpleasant memories.

A COLLECTOR

Another reason to hang on to things is the concept of collecting. My mother was always a collector; she loved antiques, old books, and just about anything else that she could get her hands on that could be subdivided into a collection.

I picked that up from her, beginning with rocks and minerals, toy soldiers, bottle caps and bits of broken colored glass. By the time I was forty, I had quite a few collections that had at one point or another in my life seemed important or worth gathering and purchasing.

Being a collector was the last barrier that I needed to confront to finish decluttering my life. Collections have emotions attached to them, usually pleasurable ones. I would never have imagined getting rid of my collection of toy soldiers, but I finally sold them off on EBay just a month ago.

CONCLUSION

Over the years and decades of our lives, many of us have collected an immense amount of objects. Most of that stuff had some value at some point, whether it be emotional, monetary, or something else. However, as the years of gone by, all they do now is weigh us down, make us depressed, and cost us money.

If you thought about it, you might be surprised to find out how much money is tied up in all of that clutter that you no longer need or want. Maybe you can put that money to better use.

Sorting Through your Clutter

There are many advantages to using EBay to help you declutter your home, but you cannot use it to sell everything. Some of your belongings will be too heavy or bulky, are or poor quality, or have suffered some kind of damage.

As you begin the adventure of decluttering your home, you should create four categories, and as you examine each object, make a decision to which it belongs in.

The first category is things that you will keep. Restrict this to the good stuff, the objects or collectibles that give you some value in your life, contribute to your survival, or help you in your current environment. The objective is to make this pile as small as possible, although you want to be careful not to throw out too much.

The second is your trash bin, which is things that are just too damaged or unsalvageable to sell anywhere.

Your third category is things that you can sell on EBay or another online selling site. I prefer EBay, but other sites such as Amazon will work fine.

And the fourth category is for objects that are too fragile, heavy or bulky to sell on EBay, or they are common or in relatively poor condition. For example, it's unwise to sell furniture on EBay because shipping can be a nightmare. These items can be donated, sold at a swap meet or thrift store, or put on sale on Craigslist (for local pickup.)

How to Begin

One of the hardest points in the decluttering adventure is the beginning. I know from experience that the first time I decided to get rid of some of my belongings was the hardest.

Decluttering is best done room by room, or closet by closet, or shelf by shelf, or some similar method. This way you can see the effects of your work as you progress.

An excellent place to start is your junk drawer. Almost everybody has a junk drawer, which is usually in the kitchen, and contains just a little bit of everything. This drawer is the place where old nuts and bolts, screws, nails, bottle caps, and hundreds of other things get put to rest because "they might be valuable someday."

After all, you never know when that old lug bolt from the car that you owned twenty years ago might save your life.

A junk drawer is generally easy to confront, because, quite literally, it's usually full of useless objects. Depending on the size of your junk collection, put aside an hour, two hours, or even a whole day, and get to work.

When I emptied my junk drawer, I laid down a piece of paper on the table to protect it from the dust, dirt, and grime. The job took about two hours, and when completed I had literally thrown out everything in the drawer. There was absolutely nothing that had any value at all.

Consider the junk drawer a practice run, a way to build up your strength in preparation for getting to the rest of your decluttering tasks. You'll find that most of the items in the drawer are obviously junk and can be thrown in the trash. At the very least if you do throw out some stuff, you'll find you have room in the drawer to collect even more junk down the road.

How to Decide

Regardless of where you are in your decluttering mission, you will be making a decision about each and every object that you come across.

For example, when decluttering my library of books, I looked at each and every book one at a time, over a period of a couple of months. For each title, I asked myself, do I keep this book? Am I ever going to read it? Am I interested in the subject? Do I like this author? And similar questions.

I wound up going through them several times because the first time through I only got rid of about 40 books. By the time I was done with the fifth pass, I had thrown out or sold over five thousand hardcover and paperback books.

Let's say you're confronting a closet which contains games and toys that you've accumulated over the years. The kids are grown up and have moved out, but you have company come over once in a while to play the games.

The idea is to examine each one and decide what to do with it. In which category – of the four listed earlier – does it belong? In this case, if the game or toy is in good condition, you can sell it on EBay. If it is in a bad condition, then you might donate it to your local Goodwill or Salvation Army, and if the condition is bad, you might just throw it away.

Sorting Through your Clutter

Keep in mind that in some cases parts of games, toys, computers and others things can also be sold on EBay. I found this out when I was looking for the game of Clue and noticed many listings for game pieces. So if your game or toy is broken or missing pieces, consider breaking it down and selling the parts or pieces individually. Search on EBay to find out if this is an option.

Going through a shelf, closet or room several times can be valuable. The first time through you're looking for the low hanging fruit, the stuff that obviously needs to be sold, donated or thrown out.

On the second pass you get rid of a little more, and on the third or even fourth time through you get rid of still more. Each time your resolve strengthens, and you wind up cutting a little deeper into the clutter.

Sometimes it's necessary to put some time between these decluttering passes of a room or area. Thus, you might declutter a closet, then move on to a cabinet in the kitchen, then a bookshelf, and then come back and declutter the first closet again.

CLEAN AS YOU GO

As I declutter each area of my home, I like to keep cleaning supplies with me, as it's an opportunity to tidy up areas that never get scrubbed down. Thus, as I'm going through my bookshelf deciding which books to keep and which to sell, I wipe down the shelves and dust off the books. That way when I'm done with that section, not only is it less cluttered, but it is fully dusted and clean.

Decluttering Room by Room

Different people have different strategies for confronting the clutter in their home. Some use a scattershot approach, meaning they bounce from room to room selling an item here and throwing out something else there without an apparent pattern.

Others, like myself, go room by room, thoroughly working from front to back and top to bottom before moving onto the next one.

Whatever your strategy, just keep working through your clutter. The key to decluttering success is to start the process, and then continue doing a little bit more regularly.

THE KITCHEN

The kitchen is one of the most used rooms of the house, second only to the bathrooms. It also tends to collect quite a bit of clutter due to the many cabinets, drawers, and organizers.

During your decluttering mission, each cabinet and drawer will be an adventure of its own. You'll find long out of date chemicals, canned foods so old they are health risks, and cooking supplies and tools so rusted they are unrecognizable.

I have found that most items in the kitchen fall into the "throw it into the trash" category, but sometimes I've been surprised to find a few salable utensils nonetheless.

Decluttering Room by Room

Unused cookware dishes still in their box, fancy mugs with writing and pictures on them, utensils in good condition, expensive dishes rarely used, and things like that are excellent to put on sale on EBay. As long as it's in reasonable shape, and easily shippable, you can sell it through that site.

In my case, I found two cooking sets each of which was missing only one pan. As a bachelor, that one pan was all that I needed. The rest of the pots and pans in the sets were in perfect, unused condition. This is the kind of stuff that might be better sold at a swap meet or yard sale, although each pan could be listed on EBay.

As I decluttered my kitchen, I found quite a few utensils, organizers, cooking tools, and other things that I had accidentally bought two or three times. Most of these were still in the original packaging. These are perfect for selling on EBay.

One of the problems with the kitchen is it is also the dirtiest room in the house, besides possibly the bathrooms. The presence of water encourages the growth of mold, mildew's and other pests while the proximity of food can attract insects, mice and so forth.

On top of that, grease spatters, crumbs and spills can cause a host of problems with any items stored in this room.

Damage can make it a challenge to find opportunities to make money by selling objects from the kitchen. They quite frequently require extra cleaning, and sometimes that is not even enough to make them ready for sale.

CLOSETS

A prime target for your decluttering efforts is any closet space. Closets tend to attract a lot more than just clothes or linen; because they are out of sight, they tend to be used to store all manner of things for extended periods of time.

Many of the things I have sold on EBay came from my closets. I've used them to store boxes of collectible items, bags of clothes, hanging costumes, camping gear, packing materials, and a host of other objects that became forgotten treasure years later.

One of the great things about closets is they tend to be dry and relatively clean. Anything stored within slowly ages and collects dust, but generally remains in salable condition.

Look through your clothes racks, find any dresses, shoes or suits in good condition that might be out of style or no longer fit. You may also find quite a few articles of clothing that no longer suit your taste. All of these are good candidates for selling on EBay. Of course, keep an eye out for any clothes that are in poor condition which should be thrown out or donated.

A walk-in closet can be a particularly lucrative location for finding salable items.

Go through every box, every drawer, all of your clothes racks, and every pile to see what you can salvage for selling on EBay, for donating, or for a yard sale.

THE GAME CLOSET

Many homes have a linen closet which has been set aside to store games of all types. This is often referred to as the game closet, and it can be a prime source of merchandise for your EBay sales.

Games sell very well on EBay, and they command good prices. For example, you remember the game Operation from many years ago? That's the one where you use a pair of tweezers to try and pull plastic bones and organs out of a body without touching the sides.

I remembered that game from when I was a child and searched on EBay because I wanted to see if I could find one. I discovered that there been many editions of this game, and the one I remembered featured a drawing of a doctor smoking while he was performing surgery. In today's politically correct world, this would be strictly forbidden, and the game cover has been changed.

Many games were made of wood or metal, and in modern times, they've been changed to use plastic parts. If you have the older games with higher quality parts, you can get good prices for them, even if they are not in perfect condition.

I was fascinated to discover that the individual plastic organs and bones from the old Operation games were being sold individually at a $1 each. I sent a few emails to the sellers, who replied that many people had those games, but the parts had been lost. In those cases, paying a dollar for a missing part salvaged a game and made it playable.

The point is that just because a game is in a bad condition doesn't mean it's entirely unsalable. The box may be crushed, and parts may be missing, but you may be able to sell the board, the cards, or other components individually.

The best way to find out is to search on EBay for each game to determine if it's popular and how it is being sold.

In fact, you might find that even if your games are in good condition, you'll make far more money selling individual pieces then you will buy putting the entire thing on sale.

Additionally, some games are no longer made at all. These could sell for quite a premium on EBay if they were popular.

Another often overlooked item that you can sell is the manuals or instruction booklets from inside a game. Rules booklets and instruction sheets tend to be lost quickly, and there are many people who are searching for them to complete their games.

If you're lucky enough to have older games from the fifties or before, you might actually have some items they can sell for quite a bit of money. Again, use EBay to research the appropriate prices to pay.

For example, a hundred years ago marbles were made of clay instead of glass. Depending on the manufacturer and style, if you have any made of clay, you might be able to sell them for more than you think.

BEDROOMS

Bedrooms often contain a wealth of potential merchandise. Because they are generally out of the sight of company and visitors, they tend to have a bit more clutter than the other rooms in the house.

This is especially true of dressers and chests of drawers, which frequently become the last resting place of hundreds or even thousands of items.

You should make a special point to go through any drawers in all your bedrooms, looking for anything that you can sell. You might be amazed at the variety of things that you find.

In most homes, you should plan on spending extra time decluttering the objects stored under the beds in the bedrooms. It's quite common for the unused space under beds to be used to store Christmas decorations, posters, artwork, and other similar things. I used to use the under bed space to store a folding table and rolled up posters, and these sold well on EBay.

CHILDREN'S BEDROOMS

Once the children have grown up or moved out, they often leave behind unneeded belongings such as toys, games, children's furniture, and clothes.

All of these items are prime merchandise that can be sold on EBay or at a yard sale, depending upon their condition. If you no longer have children in the household, then you can certainly earn some extra money by selling all of this stuff on EBay, Craigslist or your local swap meet.

Older children's toys are especially salable. Any toy that dated before the age of plastic — in other words, made of wood or metal — will generally get a good price on EBay.

Collectible toys, depending on the genre, also command a good price.

Don't forget about the junky little toys that came with happy meals or the equivalent from decades ago. Believe it or not, some people collect these things.

When I was a child, I built plastic, wood and metal models of airplanes, hot rods, spaceships, and science fiction creatures. These models are in high demand, and if you have any unbuilt in the original box, you can generally get a pretty good price.

Model builders often need parts to complete or add to their kits. For example, someone building a model car from a kit might want to exchange the tires for something flashier. These hobbyists will look on EBay to see if anyone is selling model parts, usually in bulk. So if you got a large number of model kits, and some of them are missing pieces or all thrown together in a box, consider selling them as parts rather than kits. You can search EBay to find out pricing and other information to determine if this makes sense for you.

Don't forget about comic books and older magazines as well as children's books. Some individual comic books are worth quite a bit of money, and others have at least some value. Even though the vast majority are virtually worthless, you can always combine them into lots of ten or even fifty comic books per listing. For example, if you have fifty issues of Spiderman comics, and they are worthless because they are relatively common, you could sell them in five lots of ten or even one lot of fifty for a good price.

Toy series such as Barbie dolls and matchbook cars are valuable to collectors, and you'll find buyers on EBay, as long as they are in good condition.

All of your children's furniture and supplies can be sold on EBay or at a yard sale. You may not get high prices for them, but you might earn a few extra dollars.

THE LIVING ROOM

In many homes the living room is used to entertain company, and as a result is usually cleaner than the rest of the house and contains some of the higher value items.

In my parents' house, there were two bookshelves filled with relatively rare volumes in addition to knickknacks and other cute items. They also had several antiques and kept a display case full of interesting things that they collected over their lives.

The end tables on either side of the couch had doors which could close, and because of that, they were stuffed with vast quantities of clutter. As a child, I would spend hours pawing through all of the exciting things that my mother had hidden inside those two end tables.

Because of the nature of the living room, it can be tempting to gloss over its contents while decluttering. After all, everything there is good stuff isn't it?

That's precisely the point — the items stored in the living room tend to be of higher quality and hence higher value.

Spend extra time in this room, if you have one, and be extra critical when deciding whether to keep something or sell it.

I think of knickknacks as dust magnets, and I wouldn't hesitate to list every single one of them on EBay and make a few extra dollars. Naturally, my mother, who loved knickknacks, would disagree. However, knickknacks sell very well, although not always for high prices, so consider listing them and seeing what you can get.

Obviously, any rare books are good candidates for selling. Even magazines can be sold on EBay — many people want to fill in holes in their collections of titles.

Go through any display cabinets with a critical eye. Keep the splendid, important collectibles, and sell the rest. Think of it as if you were pruning trees in the backyard. You get rid of some of the branches and leaves, so the tree looks better over time.

Make an effort to go through any drawers or cabinets or anything else where clutter can be hidden. Even in the living room, these hiding places can become filled with objects that you be better off selling, donating or throwing out.

By spending extra time decluttering your living room, you'll make an even better impression on visitors and company. Just remember that a less cluttered appearance makes a great impression on people.

THE FAMILY ROOM OR STUDIO

When I was growing up, the family room was the most important room of the home. This was where the family was gathered virtually all of the time.

Decluttering Room by Room

We had a huge console TV, a couch, an easy chair (for dad of course) and a fireplace. Virtually every night, the family could be found here, watching television, playing games, talking, and socializing.

Because of this, there was a wealth of clutter, and much of it could be salvaged and sold on EBay or at a yard sale.

As with every room, take great care to go through any drawers or cabinets. In this room, especially, these tend to fill up quickly with all manner of things.

Keep an eye out for any games which are no longer used, toys which nobody needs, posters, artwork, supplies, and so forth.

THE DINING ROOM

Many times the dining room is an extension of the living room, and as such is intended primarily for company. When I was growing up, the family always ate in the family room, because that's where the television and games were located.

Regardless of whether or not you use the dining room in everyday life, you can find may things that you can sell on EBay. This is especially true if you have a cabinet or two containing china, silverware and other utensils. If you're no longer using them, you should certainly sell them off on EBay.

BATHROOMS

The bathroom is the dirtiest, most filthy room of any house, for obvious reasons. The presence of running water and steam from showers and baths quickly degrades anything stored there.

Nonetheless, it's important to spend some time decluttering your bathrooms. You need to get rid of any old chemicals, such as cleaning fluids, floor wax, and so forth. It's a good idea to also take the time to make sure that anything hazardous is stored in such a way that it can't be accessed by children or animals.

However, you can find things that can be sold, even from a bathroom. For example, I bought an electric toothbrush which was on sale, and stored it under the sink unopened, intending to get to it in the future. I forgot about it, and three years later sold it on EBay.

It's definitely worth the time to declutter your bathrooms, even if all you achieve is to throw out some old hazardous chemicals.

STORAGE UNITS

Many people keep some of their most valuable clutter in storage units. I'm amazed by the volume of objects that people cannot bear to throw away. For some reason, some people keep everything they've ever owned, to the point where they overflow to outdoor storage cabinets and even rent whole storage units.

Some apartment complexes have small storage units, or cabinets, in the back of garages, set at just above chest high on a wall. These tend to become filled with all kinds of things that are quickly forgotten and gather dust for years. Make it a point to go through these units early in your declutter campaign. Since these cabinets are outdoors, or partially exposed to the elements, wear gloves and be on the lookout for spiders, mice, rats and other pests.

A rented storage unit is a whole other matter, and these should be confronted quickly during your declutter campaign. Rented storage units are costing you money, quite often to store things that you're never going to use again.

Thus, not only can you make money from selling off most of the items in your storage unit, you can save money by not renting one (or more) anymore.

One of my neighbors had to rent a storage unit when one of their parents passed away. They had to store her belongings somewhere, so they rented storage, intending it to be temporary until they could find something else to do with it all.

In my experience, these "temporary" storage solutions quickly become permanent. In the case of my neighbors, once they had the unit, it was so convenient that they kept adding more and more things to it until it was so full that they were looking at renting a second unit.

Decluttering a rented storage unit can take a substantial amount of time, especially if you're unsure of the contents. You don't have to confront the whole task at once. You can do it a box at a time, or start from the front and declutter a little bit each weekend.

THE GARAGE

I think the garage is a magnet for just about everything that needs to be stored. After all, it is a large space which is out-of-the-way and generally off-limits for guests and visitors. This makes it perfect to attract mountains of clutter.

When I was growing up, I did something to upset my parents – it must've been terrible – and to make up for what I'd done I had to clean out the entire garage. The job took several days, and when it was done it was clean as a whistle.

I found a rubber raft (one of those blowup kinds), boxes of tools of all type, a case of light bulbs, several old televisions, engine parts, boxes and boxes of my mother's crafting supplies, piles of art materials, and hundreds of other items. This was well before the days of the Internet, much less EBay, and I was too young to own a car, so I simply threw it all out. After all, I was told to make it so clean that you could eat off the floors.

This serves to illustrate the variety of potential merchandise that could be sitting in your garage. Make sure that it's near the top of your list of places to declutter because you could potentially get a lot of income from what is stored there.

Just be careful to wear gloves and watch out for spiders. Black widows love those dark corners, and the garage is often full of sharp pieces of metal and broken glass.

THE CAR

Believe it or not, many people store quite a few things in their cars. Sometimes the trunk of a car holds more clutter than a small closet.

Thus, as you are on your decluttering mission, don't forget to examine and declutter any automobile that you own. Check the trunk and the interior for any items that are being stored inside.

For example, when some people sell their cars, they keep the jacks and store them in the trunk of their new car. Over the years, they might have three, four or even five jacks, perhaps a pair of tire irons, and a few other things that have migrated from car to car over the years. All of these things can be sold on EBay.

While you're cleaning out the trunk, keep your eye open for things that shouldn't be there, such as cans of gasoline, containers of propane, old food and so forth like that should be removed and discarded or stored elsewhere.

ART, POSTERS AND HANDMADE ITEMS

I've always liked having art and posters hanging on my walls. There's something about having interesting images around me that makes me feel better and improves my mood.

However, as I've gotten older, my tastes have changed. The artwork and posters that I previously bought no longer appealed to me. Some of that artwork wound up stored in the closet, and the posters got rolled up, returned to their tubes, and stashed under the bed.

Artwork, mainly originals, can command an excellent price on EBay although they can take quite a bit of time to sell. Don't hesitate to put it up for sale if it no longer appeals to you.

If you have any hobbies, such as needlepoint or painting miniatures, be aware that your finished products can be sold on EBay. Painted miniatures or dolls can command quite a premium if they're well done. Framed and finished needlepoint, and even finished model kits can be sold.

Conclusion

Virtually everyone can use a little extra cash now and then, but working two or even three jobs can put a strain on a person's health, social life, and family. Wouldn't it be better if you could find a way to make some extra income while working in your pajamas in the comfort of your own home?

In this book, I've discussed one of the options you have, which is to sell off the clutter stored all over your home, in your garage, in storage units, in your backyard, and even in your car.

Most likely, this stuff was important at some time in your life, but now all of it is just sitting in boxes and not helping anyone. There may be emotional ties to these things, but it's best to move forward and put the past behind you.

In any event, it doesn't hurt to take a look through your clutter and see if there are things that you can sell using a site such as EBay.

Once you begin selling, it's best to start by confronting anything that is costing real money to store, such as in storage rental units. In these instances, not only do you get a little extra cash from selling off items that you probably don't need anymore, but you can even stop paying those expensive monthly costs for storing your junk.

There are plenty of other places to find clutter in your home. Check out dresser drawers, under the bed, closets, attic space, the garage, storage units in the backyard, and

Conclusion

anyplace else that's out of sight and out of mind. These types of places tend to accumulate junk over the years because they aren't seen, and they are very convenient.

Begin your EBay adventures by making a few small purchases to get the feel of the site and build up your feedback score. Follow that with selling a few small items that are inexpensive and easy to ship to continue your education and hone your selling skills.

After you've done that for a few weeks, jump right in and start selling. The best way to make income on eBay is to sell, then sell some more, and then sell even more. The more you have listed, the more you can sell.

Be aware of the fees and shipping costs, especially that of materials, to ensure that you don't take a loss.

Take a few minutes to read over eBay's terms and conditions thoroughly, and understand the rules you must follow as a seller. EBay can have some pretty harsh penalties for breaking these rules because they are always on guard against spammers and scammers. By understanding the rules, you can reduce the chances that you accidentally violate one of them and get penalized.

Most of all, have fun and enjoy this new adventure. Depending on the quality and quantity of items that you have to sell, you could find yourself making a good second income very quickly. You may even follow in my footsteps, and explore options for selling things purchased in thrift stores, flea markets, swap meets, from the neighbors, and so forth.

That extra income can become very useful, and if you play it right, you may find yourself being able to pay off some debts, go on a vacation, or buy a luxury that you really need and want at this moment in time.

Isn't that better than having piles of things that you no longer need, want, or even remember why you purchased in the first place stashed all over your home?

There is no better time than now to get started. Begin looking through your stuff and it should soon become obvious which items you no longer need. Use them to make that extra money today.

You'll find more information about how to work with eBay itself in the companion book to this volume called *How to Sell on eBay*. The third volume in the series, *Make Money Using the Internet to Build a Second Income and Create your Own Business,* goes into even more options for making money on the web.

Good luck, and feel free to send me an email at rich@thewritingking.com describing your progress.

Conclusion

Before you go

If you scroll to the last page in this eBook, you will have the opportunity to leave feedback and share the book with Before You Go. I'd be grateful if you turned to the last page and shared the book.

Also, if you have time, please leave a review. Positive reviews are incredibly useful. If you didn't like the book, please email me at rich@thewritingking.com and I'd be happy to get your input.

linkedin.thewritingking.com

About the Author

https://www.linkedin.com/in/richardlowejr
Feel free to send a connection request

Follow me on Twitter: @richardlowejr

Richard Lowe has leveraged more than 35 years of experience as a Senior Computer Manager and Designer at four companies into that of a bestselling author, blogger, ghostwriter, and public speaker. He has written hundreds of articles for blogs and ghostwritten more than a dozen books and has published manuscripts about computers, the Internet, surviving disasters, management, and human rights. He is currently working on a ten-volume science fiction series – the Peacekeeper Series – to be published at the rate of three volumes per year, beginning in 2016.

Richard started in the field of Information Technology, first as the Vice President of Consulting at Software Techniques, Inc. Because he craved action, after six years he moved on to work for two companies at the same time: he was the Vice President of Consulting at Beck Computer Systems and the Senior Designer at BIF Accutel. In January 1994, Richard found a home at Trader Joe's as the Director of Technical Services and Computer Operations. He remained with that incredible company for almost 20 years before taking an early retirement to begin a new life as a professional writer. He is currently the CEO of The Writing King, a company that provides all forms of writing services, the owner of The EBay King, and a Senior Branding Expert for LinkedIn Makeover. You can find a current list of all books on his Author Page and

About the Author

take a look at his exclusive line of coloring books at <u>The</u> <u>Coloring King</u>.

Richard has a quirky sense of humor and has found that life is full of joy and wonder. As he puts it, "This little ball of rock, mud, and water we call Earth is an incredible place, with many secrets to discover. Beings fill our corner of the universe, and some are happy, and others are sad, but each has their unique story to tell."

His philosophy is to take life with a light heart, and he approaches each day as a new source of happiness. Evil is ignored, discarded, or defeated; good is helped, enriched, and fulfilled. One of his primary interests is to educate people about their human rights and assist them to learn how to be happy in life.

Richard spent many happy days hiking in national parks, crawling over boulders, and peering at Indian pictographs. He toured the Channel Islands off Santa Barbara and stared in fascination at wasps building their homes in Anza-Borrego. One of his joys is photography, and he has photographed more than 1,200 belly dancing events, as well as dozens of Renaissance fairs all over the country.

Because writing is his passion, Richard remains incredibly creative and prolific; each day he writes between 5,000 and 10,000 words, diligently using language to bring life to the world so that others may learn and be entertained.

Richard is the CEO of The Writing King, which specializes in fulfilling any writing need. You can find out more at https://www.thewritingking.com/, and emails are welcome at rich@thewritingking.com

Books by Richard G Lowe Jr.

<u>Business Professional Series</u>

<u>On the Professional Code of Ethics and Business Conduct in the Workplace – Professional Ethics: 100 Tips to Improve Your Professional Life</u> - have you ever wondered what it takes to be successful in the professional world? This book gives you some tips that will improve your job and your career.

<u>Help! My Boss is Whacko! - How to Deal with a Hostile Work Environment</u> - sometimes the problem is the boss. There are all kinds of managers, some competent, some incompetent, and others just plain whacked. This book will help you understand and handle those different types of managers.

<u>Help! I've Lost My Job: Tips on What to do When You're Unexpectedly Unemployed</u> – suddenly having to leave your job can be a harsh and emotional time in your life. Learn some of the things that you need to consider and handle if this happens to you.

<u>Help! My Job Sucks Insider Tips on Making Your Job More Satisfying and Improving Your Career</u> – sometimes conditions conspire to make the regular trek to a job feel like a trip through Dante's Inferno. Sometimes, these are out of our control, such as a malicious manager or incompetent colleague. On the other hand, we can take control of our lives and workplace and improve our situation. Get this book to learn what you can do when your job sucks.

Books by Richard G Lowe Jr.

How to Manage a Consulting Project: Make money, get your project done on time, and get referred again and again – I found that being a consultant is a great way to earn a living. Managing a consulting project can be a challenge. This book contains some tips to help you so you can deliver a better product or service to your customers.

How to be a Good Manager and Supervisor, and How to Delegate – Lessons Learned from the Trenches: Insider Secrets for Managers and Supervisors – I've been a manager for over thirty years I learned many things about how to get the job done and deliver quality service. The information in this book will help you manage your projects to a high level of quality.

Focus on LinkedIn – Learn how to create a LinkedIn profile and to network effectively using the #1 business social media site.

Home Computer Security Series

Safe Computing is Like Safe Sex: You have to practice it to avoid infection – Security expert and Computer Executive, Richard Lowe, presents the simple steps you can take to protect your computer, photos and information from evil doers and viruses. Using easy-to-understand examples and simple explanations, Lowe explains why hackers want your system, what they do with your information, and what you can do to keep them at bay. Lowe answers the question: how to you keep yourself say in the wild west of the internet.

Books by Richard G Lowe Jr.

Disaster Preparation and Survival Series

Real World Survival Tips and Survival Guide: Preparing for and Surviving Disasters with Survival Skills – CERT (Civilian Emergency Response Team) trained and Disaster Recovery Specialist, Richard Lowe, lays out how to make you, your family, and your friends ready for any disaster, large or small. Based upon specialized training, interviews with experts and personal experience, Lowe answers the big question: what is the secret to improving the odds of survival even after a big disaster?

Creating a Bug Out Bag to Save Your Life: What you need to pack for emergency evacuations - When you are ordered to evacuate—or leave of your free will—you probably won't have a lot of time to gather your belongings and the things you'll need. You may have just a few minutes to get out of your home. The best preparation for evacuation is to create what is called a bug out bag. These are also known as go-bags, as in, "grab it and go!"

Professional Freelance Writer Series

How to Operate a Freelance Writing Business, and How to be a Ghostwriter – Proven Tips and Tricks Every Author Needs to Know about Freelance Writing: Insider Secrets from a Professional Ghostwriter – This book explains how to be a ghostwriter, and gives tips on everything from finding customers to creating a statement of work to delivering your final product.

How to Write a Blog That Sells and How to Make Money From Blogging: Insider Secrets from a Professional Blogger:

Books by Richard G Lowe Jr.

Proven Tips and Tricks Every Blogger Needs to Know to Make Money – There is an art to writing an article that prompts the reader to make a decision to do something. That's the narrow focus of this book. You will learn how to create an article that gets a reader interested, entices them, informs them, and causes them to make a decision when they reach the end.

Other Books by Richard Lowe Jr

How to Be Friends with Women: How to Surround Yourself with Beautiful Women without Being Sleazy – I am a photographer and frequently find myself surrounded by some of the most beautiful women in the world. This book explains how men can attract women and keep them as friends, which can often lead to real, fulfilling relationships.

How to Throw Parties like a Professional: Tips to Help You Succeed with Putting on a Party Event – Many of us have put on parties, and I know it can be a daunting and confusing experience. In this book, I share what I learned from hosting small house parties to shows and events.

Additional Resources

Is your career important to you? Find out how to move your career in any direction you desire, improve your long-term livelihood, and be prepared for any eventuality. Visit the page below to sign up to receive valuable tips via email, and to get a free eBook about how to optimize your LinkedIn profile.

http://list.thewritingking.com/

I've written and published many books on a variety of subjects. They are all listed on the following page.

https://www.thewritingking.com/books/

On that site, I also publish articles about business, writing, and other subjects. You can visit by clicking the following link:

https://www.thewritingking.com

To find out more about me or my photography, you can visit these sites:

Personal website: https://www.richardlowe.com
Photography: http://www.richardlowejr.com
LinkedIn Profile: https://www.linkedin.com/in/richardlowejr
Twitter: https://twitter.com/richardlowejr

If you have any comments about this book, feel free to email me at rich@thewritingking.com

Premium Writing Services

Do you have a story that needs to be told? Have you been trying to write a book for ages but never can seem to find the time to get it done? Do you want to brand your business, but don't know how to get started?

The Writing King has the answer. We can help you with any of your writing needs.

Ghostwriting. We can write your book, which entails interviewing you to get your story, writing the book and then working with you to revise it until complete. To discuss your book, contact The Writing King today.

Website Copy. Many businesses include the text on their sites as an afterthought, and that can result in lost sales and leads. Hire The Writing King to review your site and recommend changes to the text which will help communicate your message and improve your sales.

Blogging. Build engagement with your customers by hiring us to write a weekly or semi-weekly article for your blog, LinkedIn or other social media. Contact The Writing King today to discuss your blogging needs.

LinkedIn. LinkedIn is of the most important vehicles for finding new business, and a professionally written profile works to pulling in those leads. Write or update your profile today.

Technical Writing. We have broad experience in the computer, warehousing and retail industries, and have

Premium Writing Services

written hundreds of technical documents. Contact <u>The Writing King</u> today to find out how we can help you with your technical writing project.

<u>The Writing King</u> has the skills and knowledge to help you with any of your writing needs. Call us today to discuss how we can help you.

www.ingramcontent.com/pod-product-compliance
Lightning Source LLC
Chambersburg PA
CBHW060244230326
41458CB00094B/1424